650.14

THE
WORK
BOOK

How to Build Your Personal Brand
and
GET HIRED!

BILL HOBBS

The La Plata Press
La Plata, MD

This book, or parts thereof, offers suggestions believed to be helpful and useful based upon the author's experience and research. Nothing in this book should be considered to be an absolute statement about a specific course of action to be taken in any particular circumstance, as numerous factors must be considered.

ISBNs: 978-0-9858456-2-9 (Paperback)
978-0-9858456-3-6 (Hard Cover)
978-0-9858456-4-3 (E-Book)

For More Information About

The WORK Book

Books, Learning Materials, and Lecture Series

www.theworkbookseries.com

Executive Editor Charles Hobbs

WHEN I FIRST RELEASED *The WORK Book* two-years ago, I never expected the world to embrace it so readily. I thought maybe a few people would read it and find a use for it. Within the first year several top colleges and universities were using and recommending the book.

Last year we launched a campaign called "Reach Students Earlier." The campaign motivated several two-year institutions and the first Statewide Public High School System to begin using *The WORK Book* to increase student employment readiness.

It's been a fun ride so far and we're excited about the future. We have two more books in the *WORK Book Series* that are currently being written. If you are interested in what's next, check out bill-hobbs.com for updates.

Included are some of the quotes from those who like the book and found it useful either in their own career searches or for helping others with their pursuit of finding a dream job.

"*The WORK Book* is now my # 1 resource when speaking with young people about their future. The exercises in the book provide a great opportunity to jump start the career planning process no matter what level. I highly recommend this resource to students as they begin the career planning process."

— *Marchelle S. Horner, Education Consultant; Career Development at PrimeTYME Consulting, LLC*

"Bill's book condenses the career journey from exploration to on the job success. A versatile tool for both college students and career changers!"

— *Patrick Devanney, Manager, Wellspring Educational Resource Center at Wellspring House*

"I work with a large population of military and veterans. Often our military members are preparing to make the transition to civilian employment and have not previously had to prepare a resume, or cover letter, or interview for a job.

Beyond that, they often have not taken time for self-reflection which is vital for building a brand and getting hired in the right job. I find the exercises in *The WORK Book* to be great starting points for coaching conversations. *The WORK Book* is a great tool for self-guided career preparation or as a complement to career advisor assistance. Bill's book is a valuable resource for any Career Coach and is an asset to any Career Center."

— *Tanya White-Earnest, Director, Career Services at Trident University International*

"*The WORK Book* is easy to understand and work through with actual examples. Practice questions and reflective exercises offered in the book allow you to quickly think about your brand and what you can bring to the table, as well as what you need to do to be successful in your career goals."

— *Sabira Vohra, Director Career Services and Planning at Stevenson University*

"Bill has elected to share his experiences as an accomplished sales leader in Fortune 500 enterprises with the broader public through his insightful *The WORK Book*. Not only does Bill convey practical advice about how to stand out and get noticed by recruiters through personal branding, he follows it up with additional, sage advice about how to influence others and position his readers for promotions. *The WORK Book* is a book that I have recommended to the students I work with and one in which I refer back to frequently."

— *Rob Liddell, Director of Career Planning at Saint Leo University*

"*The WORK Book* has been a valuable resource in our undergraduate career education curriculum, with straightforward advice that complements the information we share in advising sessions. Bill Hobbs provides a practical approach and easy to follow suggestions to improve a student's marketability and competitiveness."

— *Mark Brostoff, Associate Dean and Director of Weston Career Center, Olin Business School at Washington University in St. Louis*

"This book makes an excellent graduation present as each member of this years' graduating class at the Rutgers Business School, New Brunswick Campus will find out! I hope you read this book and apply its concepts to help you find that first placement and again and again as your career progresses."

— *Eugene C. Gentile, Director,*
Office of Career Management,
Undergraduate New Brunswick and
Specialty Masters Programs at
Rutgers Business School

"I believe that this book is great for career professionals if they want a user guide for students enrolled in a career development class, a senior year experience program or capstone event. The activities allow a professional to guide students through awareness-building exercises and give the students the gift of processing that they rarely spend time doing as they transition from college to career."

— *Meghan Lynn Godorov,*
Associate Director for Alumnae
and Community Engagement at
Mount Holyoke College

"Career development professionals will find this book offers a comprehensive step-by-step decision making process that encompasses the more personal side of the career transition, including such issues as self-awareness, money matters, branding, sourcing leads, interviewing and best practices in a new position.

Clients can learn about what they, as job seekers, are going to face at every step in the job search process that collectively can have an impact on their success. The author defines and provides a real world view for career information and decision-making. For example, preparedness is the key take-away throughout the book as well as to always expect the unexpected — again offering advice that a career practitioner would offer a client. The book will be especially helpful for any job seeker who wants a quick overview and to review the high points of the career planning process and job search techniques. It could also be used as a practical reminder throughout anyone's career. The most useful information is how to create a strong personal brand, the process of securing the job offer, and how to elevate personal brand once in the position."

— *Liane H. Gould, Manager of*
Adult Services at Arlington County

Excerpted from "The WORK Book Book Review," by Liane H. Gould, which appeared in NCDA's web magazine, Career Convergence, at www.ncda.org. Copyright © August/2013.

Reprinted with permission.

CONTENTS

INTRODUCTION

I BEGAN MY CAREER in the Fortune 500 world, first as an Account Executive and later as a business manager specializing in turnarounds and new market expansions. About ten years later, I made the transition to the world of startups and eventually began advising other CEOs of growth stage companies how to navigate strategic and tactical elements of their businesses. I truly enjoy the business world and building successful teams.

I began writing *The WORK Book Series* a few years ago after I was invited to talk to college students about my experiences in business. Students would often ask me during Q&A sessions to recommend books that would help them prepare for a career after graduation.

I wanted to recommend a book that took a holistic approach to personal branding, one that promoted collaboration with Career Services and faculty advisors, and one that included exercises to help students prepare for the difficulties of the hiring process. I found that the book I wanted to recommend didn't exist. I created *The WORK Book* to address students' current and future needs in the job market. Since professional growth and building a personal brand are continuous processes that are highly effective for career advancement, this book also helps students grow after they find a new career. *The WORK Book Series* addresses all of these needs and is short enough that students can read it quickly and apply it immediately.

Career services can help you to format a complete résumé. We, however, will focus on ensuring that the content and experience is representative of your true brand value.

Even if you land an interview, these same hiring managers may spend little time preparing before your interview. They may only glance at your résumé and do a quick digital search right before meeting with you. If your brand presence is weak, then you will miss an important opportunity to impress the manager with your unique value before your interview.

A lot of books focus their content on the interview, framing it as the "most important part of the process." Interviews are critically important, but they are only a small part of the hiring process. You can build your brand in a way that says great things about you long before you ever sit down for an interview, and your unique personal brand can help to accelerate your progress long after you are hired.

The digital world is a warehouse of information about each of us, making it very important to understand, shape, and manage your digitally available information and messaging. I have heard a lot of stories about people who have lost opportunities because of the information that a simple search revealed. Be aware that anything you post, write, or comment could be seen by the entire world.

On the positive side, if you are open to producing content that enhances your personal brand, the digital world can provide you some amazing opportunities.

Building a digital presence around your personal brand can be fun and rewarding. The idea is to create and maintain a portfolio of your work that illustrates why you are unique and what value you bring to a business or industry. This presence is a blend of your unique skills, background, education, the industry knowledge you have, and your related areas of interest.

A good first step is to ensure that you have a presence on social media that connects to your field of interest. With your professional social media, it is important to be honest and upfront while you build an engaged network of collaborators and industry professionals. This network can help you learn, grow, and even find new opportunities.

Creating your own website is another way to improve your brand. A professional website can become a central point of reference for your personal brand. It allows you to more easily control messaging about who you are professionally, display your work and projects, display your successes and partnerships, and create a single thread to tie together your related professional interests.

From your website, you can link to other sites where you have built elements of your overall brand presence. For example, if you are working toward becoming a professional writer and you love cooking, you might begin a blog that links back to a website you have created on cooking. Both sites would showcase your writing skills and build on additional elements of your brand. You may even become a contributor for a digital publisher that already has a great presence and, if permitted, link back to your website.

Other elements of your brand that don't directly relate to your field of interest but illustrate your commitment to learning and growing professionally can also be utilized to display your depth to prospective employers. For example, if you are a painter, a tutor, or you design jewelry in your free time but want to land a career in management consulting, showing progress in these areas may not obviously connect; however, your success in these fields can contribute to your brand. Furthermore, they help to paint a picture of your interests and accomplishments while revealing an interesting and fun side of your personal brand, thus separating you from other candidates.

Career Services and Faculty Advisors are your Best Resources

As you read *The WORK Book*, remember the best resources for developing your personal brand are Career Services and faculty advisors. If you begin building relationships with these professionals early on, they can guide you as you choose classes and build skill sets that will set you apart long after you graduate. These professionals have great experience and can help you shape your raw ideas into a finely tuned personal brand.

Because in many colleges and universities the number of students eclipses the number of Career Services and faculty advisors, there will always be constraints on the amount of time each student has with his or her resources. Prepare yourself by bringing ideas and answers that you develop as you work through the following sections to your meetings with them. This will allow you to get the most out of your discussions with Career Services and your faculty advisors. The relationships, experience, and interactive collaboration can prove invaluable as you build your personal brand.

When I began writing this book, I spent time talking with some of the Career Services personnel I worked with as an employer, and I also reached out to faculty advisors that had helped me when I was in school. The biggest challenge I heard repeatedly was getting students to engage with their professional resources as early as possible. The sooner you engage with these assets, the sooner the faculty advisors and Career Services teams can begin to collaboratively work with you to create a powerful plan for success.

Whether it's the first time or the fifteenth time you are looking to build a new career, the process and philosophy remains constant: never stop growing!

CHAPTER TWO

THE JOURNEY

BEGINNING A NEW CAREER can conjure a mixture of emotions. The prospect of financial independence and the realization that you will soon embark on a new journey in life can be exciting and a little overwhelming, all at once. To become truly happy and subsequently successful in your new career, you will need to spend a little time to truly understand yourself, the process, and the employers you will meet along the way. In less than two hours, you can read this guidebook and begin to apply the concepts to your new journey. It is normal to feel some apprehension and anxiety along with the anticipation and excitement. If you approach this new experience with an open mind and a clear understanding of what you really want to accomplish, the apprehension and anxiety will begin to melt away. It all starts with identifying the right career path. Choosing a career path that interests you and allows you to learn, develop, and grow as a professional, can make a big difference in your overall happiness and ability to succeed.

CHAPTER THREE

CHOICES

WHEN YOU FIRST DECIDE it's time to find a new career, there are many factors to consider. You should start with the big picture elements and then work down to the smaller, more detailed elements. Choosing which field to pursue is the first step in the process and should be completed before considering other factors such as where to live, compensation, and schedule.

Below is a quick worksheet to help you channel your thoughts. Often, seeing things on paper helps to clarify ideas and solidify choices. Think through each section, and write your answers.

If you are planning to enter a technical field like accounting, engineering, or law, then you have already chosen your field. However, you may want to narrow down the job type or even industry. For instance, whether you enjoy financial planning or auditing will determine the type of accounting careers you should go after. If you are undecided on the type of field to enter, you should first spend some time reflecting on your interests, previous experience, education, and general skills. It's important to choose a field that is interesting and exciting to you but is also well aligned with your skill set. If you enjoy meeting new people and solving business problems, you may enjoy sales, consulting, or public relations. If you enjoy strategy and analytics, then you might enjoy business strategy, business analytics, or business operations.

Once you have chosen a field, you need to consider the career options available to you in that field. Read job descriptions within that field, and consider whether you could see yourself in that position. Spend a little time on the internet finding out what types of jobs are available and where the highest concentrations of those jobs are available.

Some jobs will be available everywhere, but other job types like manufacturing, IT, or Import/ Export jobs will have hubs where large concentrations of a particular job type exist.

As you work through your options, you should consider what additional resources you have that could be helpful during your search. A great place to start is your career center. Whether you are a current student or an alumnus who has been out of school for a while, you likely have access to a career counselor. Career counselors often have a broader range of search resources at their disposal and often have a large network of hiring managers who they interface with on a regular basis. They also keep in contact with alumni who are looking for candidates from time to time and may be able to provide a warm introduction. Take some time to walk through your goals and share your worksheet with your career counselor so that you both understand the factors affecting your decision.

Use the rest of the worksheet to work through other factors of consideration.

► What fields are most interesting to me?

A. _____

B. _____

C. _____

D. _____

E. _____

► What types of positions are available in these fields given my level of experience?

A. _____

B. _____

C. _____

D. _____

E. _____

▶ Which industries most appeal to me?

    A. _____

    B. _____

    C. _____

    D. _____

    E. _____

▶ What types of positions (titles) or job requirements fit my level of experience and skill set?

    A. _____

    B. _____

    C. _____

    D. _____

    E. _____

▶ Where are the majority of these opportunities located?

A. _____

B. _____

C. _____

D. _____

E. _____

▶ Am I able to live in the areas with high concentrations of opportunities?

☐ Yes   ☐ No   ☐ Maybe

▶ If not, can I work remotely?

☐ Yes   ☐ No   ☐ Maybe

▶ What are my long term career goals?

A. _____

B. _____

C. _____

D. _____

E. _____

▶ Is this type of career a financially viable option for me right now?

☐ Yes   ☐ No   ☐ Maybe

▶ How can I better prepare myself to increase my chances of securing employment?

A. _____

B. _____

C. _____

D. _____

E. _____

As you write down the answers to these questions, consider how the answers affect your decision. If you are really serious about working in a particular field, you will need to make up your mind that you are going to give one-hundred percent to your new career. You will need to master new skills and continuously reevaluate your progress.

CHAPTER FOUR
MONEY MATTERS

WHEN SPEAKING WITH PEOPLE who want to change jobs or are first-time job seekers, the question about money often arises. "Should money really be a factor in my decision?" The answer to the question is really one that each person needs to make on his or her own. Every journey is a little different, and individual circumstances do affect career decisions.

When I began my first full-time career search after college, I decided to find a career that aligned well with my experience, education, and skill set. I interviewed with companies across a broad range of industries because I didn't know yet what type of industry would be the most interesting to me.

By the end of the interview process, I had chosen to take a consultative selling job in the IT industry. To my surprise, once I had a strong résumé, reached out to hiring managers, and got comfortable interviewing, each company spent time selling me on their company and industry. I chose the company and industry where I felt I had the most potential for success and career growth.

During the six-month process of researching, interviewing, negotiating, and deciding on a company, a friend asked me, "What would you do if money didn't matter?" I thought for a minute and replied, "I would probably be a writer."

She said, "Then that is your passion, and you should go for it!"

I smiled and said, "But writers don't make any money unless they are really, really successful."

"Yes, but if that is your passion, you should forget about everything else and do it!"

In a society where money doesn't matter, she would have been exactly right. Unfortunately for me, the lenders who gave me the money for my education didn't feel the same way. I owed sixty thousand dollars and needed to pay for an apartment and a car, plus have money left over to eat each month, so writing books was not an option for me at the time. The consultative selling job I took helped me to gradually pay down my school loans and allowed me to spend some time writing on weekends. Am I disappointed that I didn't follow my dream immediately? No, that was not really what I wanted; I wanted to enjoy a comfortable lifestyle, and I enjoyed working with different types of people which I was able to do as a sales consultant in the business world.

When writing was a fantasy, it sounded great. I could sit down and write every day, but I had never really taken the time to consider everything else that came with it and all the "real" work. There was the "branding" of the book and building a platform. There was the selling of the idea to book agents, publishers, and PR reps. Then there was the need to sell speaking engagements, book talks, and book signings. All of this was the "stuff" I had failed to consider when I fell in love with the idea of writing. The skills I learned through practicing business and selling prepared me to better understand what the aforementioned people do. After all, they are all selling a product as well. And this understanding allowed me to interact with them in a more meaningful way.

I do believe that people should follow their dreams, but it is critical to truly understand what it takes to accomplish them. Jumping into something new and just hoping it will work out, is not a good idea. The best way to ultimately realize your dreams is to take a little time to think through what you really want, understand what it will take, and formulate a plan to help you achieve those dreams.

CHAPTER FIVE

FIT FIRST

WHAT IS MOST IMPORTANT throughout the interview process is developing a mutual understanding. You want to really understand the company you will be working for, and they want to really understand who you are and how you will fit into their company.

Going into an interview with a "win the job" mindset is not the right approach. Always consider the long term. Winning the job is the easy part. Keeping the job and building a successful career is much more difficult. Mutual understanding is the most important building block in determining "fit."

The ability to build a successful career depends on a lot of factors, but the first and most important factor to your success is "fit." "Fit" is a term that describes the way you will align with a company's strategy, structure, and culture. You definitely don't want to win the job at the wrong company because you could end up bored out of your mind, stressed out, hating the company culture, or getting shipped off to some place you really don't want to be.

"Fit" is very important to the employer as well. The last thing an employer wants is to hire you and spend thousands of dollars and countless hours training you just to have you quit in six months because the job wasn't what you expected. Good employers pay close attention to "fit" in order to provide employees the best chance for long-term success.

For example, if you like to wake up at 9 am, begin the day by 10:30 am and work until 7:30 or 8, then a job that starts at 8 am and requires you to work until 5 pm may not be a good "fit" for you. Or if you like to work from home but the company requires you to work in an office cubicle environment, then the job may not be a good "fit" for you.

The search for the right fit begins long before the face-to-face interview. Employers search for referral applicants, scan résumés, hire professional recruiters, and check references. This helps them increase their chances for success. You must maximize your chances for success and happiness with a new company as well. Begin your research early, and don't let yourself just "settle" because you will waste valuable time doing something that doesn't make you happy. As we discussed in the previous chapter, spend some time talking with a career counselor to see if he or she can help you with any possible leads for companies and hiring managers that fit your search.

Also, be sure to look at your existing contacts and social media to see if there are any existing relationships that can help you find potential employers.

Career fairs are another way to meet a lot of potential employers and learn about their companies in a short period of time. The face-to-face aspect of the career fair gives you an opportunity to talk with potential hiring managers and build your network. If you make a great impression with them at the job fair, it's reasonable to believe that you will have a better chance of securing a follow-up interview. Be sure to immediately email any companies you liked, thank them for the time, and ask about a follow-up interview.

Don't forget to look back at the questions you answered in the previous chapter. Spend some additional time researching, and make a list of all the companies that fit the description of what you are looking for. Then locate job openings that are available within each company and note the link to the listing on the worksheet below.

List of Potential Companies with Job openings

Company   **Website or Job Link**

1. Company A   www.abcdefg123.com/jobopening/USA

2. Company B   _____

3. Company C   _____

4. Company D   _____

5. Company E _____

6. Company F _____

Now, prioritize the openings in order from your top to least favorite options.

Order of Companies from First to Last Choice Example

Rank   Company Name

  1.   Company D

  2.   Company G

  3.   Company A

  4.   Company F

  5.   Company B

  6.   Company E

  7.   Company C

Order of Companies from First Choice to Last Choice Worksheet

Rank	Company Name
1.	_____
2.	_____
3.	_____
4.	_____
5.	_____
6.	_____

Now you have a target list and know exactly what is available. Set that list aside for a moment, and be sure that you are actually ready to begin applying. You need to understand that everything you do regarding your career is a representation of you. You are your own brand, and your brand either gains value or loses value based on your choices. New employers know very little about you and will view you based on the limited data points they have. If you have a great résumé, great references, and you spend some time developing a good rapport before the interview, employers will be more likely to view your brand as valuable and hire you. This is because they can only base their initial opinion of you on these things. Conversely, if you have a poorly written résumé, no references, and have never spoken to any of the interviewers, employers will base their initial opinion of you on your poorly written résumé. They will not even waste the time to check your references or give you an interview.

CHAPTER SIX

REPRESENTATIVE RÉSUMÉS

A RÉSUMÉ IS THE FIRST representation of you and your brand that any employer will see. It is critical that the résumé looks professional and includes all of the necessary contacts and work history, but your résumé should be much more than that. Since employers are looking through thousands of résumés at a time, many use word searches to narrow the pool into a smaller group with reasonably similar skill sets. For example, if you want to be hired as a landscape architect, there might be some key words like "Landscape", "Architect", "Designer", "Natural", "Outdoor", "Trees", etc. that the employer looks for electronically in the stack of résumés. They may then look for specific certifications, education background, or experience requirements to further narrow the pool. After that, someone will need to read each of the remaining résumés and look for possible candidates to interview over the phone or in person. Once your résumé is in someone's hands, it will need to attract his or her attention. This means that your résumé should not only look professional and be formatted properly but that it should address the skill set that employers are searching for. One way to find some of the skills that are important for a specific job type is to look at job postings online. In the requirements section of a job posting, companies will detail the skills required for that type of position. If you look at ten to fifteen examples, themes will start to emerge. For example, if you were wanting to become a manager for a tech company, some of the postings you look at will say things like, "experience managing people", "familiarity with CRM software", "three years minimum in the field of...", "excellent communication skills", and "ability to provide meaningful feedback".

From these listings, you can glean words or skills that are applicable to include in your résumé. The key is to arrange the words in a way that highlights the skills you have with the work you have done. For example,

▸ If you were a supervisor at a retail store but did not have the three years of management experience, you could still highlight your experience as a supervisor and include the results you achieved over a period of time. For example you might say, "Exceeded in store revenue targets by an average of twenty-two percent while supervising a team of four store associates during a two and a half year period of time."

▸ If you were a bartender in school and the requirement is good communication skills, you might say, "Built strong relationships with regular customers and created new customer loyalty by leveraging strong interpersonal communication skills as a bartender."

In either example you may not have the exact skills outlined in the requirements section, but you can highlight the skills and experience that you do have that make you a strong candidate.

Another important element to a strong résumé is the story that your various jobs tell. If you were a store clerk and then were promoted to a supervisor, or a bartender and then given additional responsibility as a bar manager, you should note that. Many people's résumés lack a story. Some people will simply list the company and the time they worked there without properly documenting the progression that occurred during their tenure. The story is important, and employers want to know that you made progress in whatever job you were doing.

The last thing I will say about résumés is to include results-oriented information that details your accomplishments in a quantifiable format. "Increased sales" means very little. "Managed a team" also means very little. What is more meaningful is a quantifiable result and how you got there. For example, "Increased sales by 200 percent over a six-month period by analyzing customer metrics and adjusting product mix to meet demand" sounds much better than "increased sales."

Another example would be, "Successfully supervised a team of associates winning the company's award of excellence for implementing new motivational strategies that improved productivity by thirty-five percent." This sounds better than "managed teams."

It is important to be sure that your résumé tells a story about work-related accomplishments and that it is professional and results-oriented. Take some time to survey the skills needed before creating your résumé, and be sure to get help at a career service center or from a professional résumé company if possible.

CHAPTER SEVEN

REACHING OUT

Now THAT YOU HAVE DECIDED on the field, have a list of possible employment opportunities, and have completed a representative résumé, it is time for you to start the application process. Be sure to build a list of point of contacts (POCs) for the various companies you are interested in. They can be hiring managers or HR representatives listed in the job posting, employees you met at career fairs, alumni who can help you better understand the company through informational interviews, or mutual, professional social media connections.

If the POC is directly involved with the hiring process, try to get in touch with him or her to confirm receipt of your résumé. If not, you can approach with more general questions (e.g. company culture, career paths, etc.) and ask for 15 minutes from his or her busy schedules for an informational interview.

Remember to research the company as well as the POC (if he or she is available) online. POCs may have limited time to talk with you, but they will appreciate your knowledge of the company and the follow-up. While you are on the phone, ask a couple of meaningful questions that you have prepared before the call about the company such as

> ▸ I noticed that your company has locations in 35 countries around the globe. What percentage of the overall revenue of the company is derived from the location where I would be working?

> ▸ A strong training program is an important factor in my choice of company. Can you tell me a little about your program?

> ▸ I noticed that your business has continued to expand in North America over the past three years. What is the primary driver of that growth?

Questions that show employers you have taken the time to research their business, understand basic concepts, and formulated meaningful questions can be very helpful in setting you apart from other candidates. You should avoid asking too many questions over the phone, but two or three well-planned, well-placed questions may help you to stand out from other applicants.

List of Strong Questions

1. _____

2. _____

3. _____

4. _____

5. _____

6. _____

7. _____

Be sure during the call to emphasize your desire to meet with them and see if they will commit to a date to meet. The little bit of extra time spent with a POC can make a big difference. This approach can also save you some time particularly in the case where there may be an old job posting that has already been filled. Talking to someone live is almost always a good idea.

CHAPTER EIGHT

FACE TO FACE

INTERVIEWS GIVE YOU an opportunity to represent yourself as something other than just a piece of paper in a stack of résumés. The process of interviewing can be a little uncomfortable the first few times, but with a little practice you can begin to build your confidence and increase your comfort with the process. Your initial interviewing should begin several months in advance of your actual expected start date. Don't wait until you really need to have a job to start interviewing. Starting early will allow you to be more selective with companies and offers, and it can reduce the amount of stress you feel from needing to get a job. Many companies have long interviewing processes where you will need to interview several times with several different people as they narrow the pool of applicants.

When you begin applying to companies, you want to apply to as many viable companies as you can, thus increasing your chances of getting multiple interviews and allowing you to develop your confidence and come across as a stronger candidate.

Once you start getting calls to set up interviews, you have a decision to make. Some companies will decide exactly when you need to come in to interview, and others will allow you to set a day and time. If you have the option, start with your least favorite options first so that you can practice during your first few interviews. This way, by the time you get to your top picks, you are well practiced and prepared for the questions they will have for you.

Before you are interviewed, be sure to familiarize yourself with current events, news associated with the company you are interviewing with, and the latest industry trends. Staying current will show that you are a well-rounded and knowledgeable candidate who is capable of discussing a variety of topics.

Dress professionally. Overdressed is always best to show that you are taking the interview seriously. Be sure to have a firm handshake and look everyone in the eye. Smile when you meet them and when you are leaving. As stated in the previous chapter, "fit" is the most important aspect of the interview process. In order to prepare ahead of time, you can read a few books that cover interviewing techniques and the typical questions interviewers ask.

Remember, you are selling yourself and building your personal brand, so be confident, truthful, and enthusiastic. Let the interviewer lead the interview, and don't talk too much. It is ok if there is silence at different periods of time. Be prepared to discuss your experience in previous jobs and relate that experience to what you will be doing at this new job. It is most important to come across as "human." If all of your answers sound canned, the interviewer will know that you are just accustomed to interviewing and you won't really stand out. If you are able to tie skills together with experience and your interests, you will be much more memorable.

Many interviews are boring, and both the interviewer and the interviewee seem to be just going through the motions. This is not productive for either side. It is critically important that you "connect" with the interviewer and create a mutual understanding. This will help you establish a basis to evaluate "fit."

Interviews are unpredictable. Knowing exactly what will be asked is impossible, but understanding some of the basic categories of questions will allow you to think about your answers ahead of time. Being prepared with examples can be very helpful in moving an interview along at a reasonable pace, but you don't want to sound rehearsed which we will discuss in the next chapter.

During the interview, you will need to listen closely to each question and be able to offer an example that demonstrates the skill set the interviewer is seeking. The goal of the interviewer's questions is to help you and the interviewer better understand each other and connect in a more meaningful way. We will discuss connecting in detail in the next chapter, so for now, just focus on effectively handling questions that might arise during the interview.

The typical types of questions an interviewer will ask in a non-technical interview should fit into one of a few categories. While this list is in no way comprehensive, we will cover a few common question-types and examples. Spend additional time before each interview thinking about other questions you may be asked. If the interview is for a technical position or a field in which you are an expert, expect questions that cover the technical elements of your specific field of expertise.

Question Types

Opening Questions: These questions open the interview and are designed to "break the ice."

▸ How was the traffic on the way here?

▸ How is the weather outside today?

▸ Did you have a good flight?

▸ Did you see what the market did this morning?

▶ Have you been following the ____ in the news?

Tip: So that you won't be surprised in the first few minutes of the interview, it's important to be calm and comfortable when you walk in the door. Take some time to review the company website again, and be sure you are familiar with the company's background and business. You should also spend a few minutes looking at the interviewers' professional social media and any articles where they are quoted. This will allow you to better understand who you will be meeting. Also, check the company website for any updates, news, or press releases that you may be able to discuss during the interview.

In addition to company news, be familiar with national and global current events and general local news. This will provide you with some other possible topics to discuss during the opening of the interview.

If you are asked about a topic that you are not familiar with, don't fake it. Just let the interviewer know that you aren't familiar with the subject and move on.

Plan to arrive early to the interview, and be sure you know how to get there. Arriving early will give you some time to calm down and relax before meeting the interviewers. If you are concerned about traffic or are unfamiliar with the area, you can leave early, drive to the location of the interview first, and then find a coffee shop or restaurant to wait in until it is time for you to interview.

Transition Questions: These questions are designed as a segue to the more focused questions throughout the rest of the interview.

► How did you hear about the job opening?

► Tell us what you know about our company?

► What interests you about working here?

► What makes you an ideal candidate for this job?

► Did anyone discuss with you in detail the responsibilities of the job we are looking to fill?

Tip: Some of the questions about the company you will have answered by doing your pre-interview research, but be sure to take a second look at the job description before the interview. After re-reading the job description, think about why you are a good candidate for the job and how your experience specifically relates to this job. You may want to print out the job description and list out the reasons you are a great candidate next to each requirement.

If you have an initial phone interview prior to the actual face-to-face interview, be sure to ask the caller for a detailed description of the job and ask them to explain the daily responsibilities. You can also ask phone interviewers to describe their "perfect candidate." Having someone answer these questions for you ahead of time will allow you to better organize your thoughts for the Transition Questions.

Experience/ Basic Knowledge: These questions focus on skill sets and basic knowledge as well as employment experience.

► Walk me through your résumé.

- ▶ Tell me about your role and responsibilities in your last job.

- ▶ Tell me about your computer and software knowledge.

- ▶ What experience do you have in the field of _____?

- ▶ How do your studies relate to this position?

- ▶ With very little experience in our industry, what skills can you bring to this new role that will help you to be successful?

Tip: You already took the time to write an impactful résumé which helped to get you the face-to-face interview. Be sure that you take some time to practice verbalizing the answers to these questions. This is your opportunity to present your value to the company in person, so your answers need to be clear and concise. Remember to directly relate your experience and achievements to the requirements of the new position. Just like you did on the résumé, be sure to describe the results you achieved in your previous jobs and how the same skills can help you to be successful in this new role.

Behavioral Questions and Teamwork: The goal of these questions is to understand how you will deal with basic instruction, stress, adversity, feedback, etc.

- ▸ Tell me about a time when you had a tough client issue that you were able to resolve.

- ▸ Tell me about your favorite job, and why you liked it.

- ▸ Tell me about your least favorite job, and why you disliked it.

- ▸ Tell me about a conflict with another employee, what happened, and how you resolved it.

- ▸ Tell me about a time when you helped improve a process within your company, and what prompted you to come up with this solution?

► Tell me about a time when you managed a team that was successful and what you did to ensure success.

► Tell me about a time when you were a part of a team that was unsuccessful. Why were they unsuccessful, and what did you learn from the experience?

Tip: Now that you understand the goal of the Behavioral Questions, spend some time before the interview picking some stories from your previous experiences where you demonstrated strong qualities that had a positive impact on your job performance. If you are newer to the job market and don't have work examples, you can use examples from school. Often classroom-based group projects, school club organizations, or sports activities will provide some good examples.

Keep your answers clear, concise, positive, and results-oriented. Focus on the facts and not the emotion, particularly if you are describing a conflict situation that you were able to resolve. Remember the focus of these questions is to help the interviewer better understand your capabilities to overcome obstacles and turn negative situations into positive situations. Be sure that your examples demonstrate these abilities.

Strengths and Weaknesses: These questions are designed to discover your strengths and weaknesses.

▸ Tell me your top three strengths.

▸ Tell me your top three weaknesses.

▸ How will these strengths factor into this new role?

▸ How might the weaknesses prevent your success in this role?

▸ What skill improvements will you need to make if you are hired into this role?

▸ What skills do you possess that will help you to be successful in this role?

Tip: Many people struggle with Strength and Weakness questions. Everyone has strengths and weaknesses. A single attribute can be either a strength or a weakness, depending on the specifics of a given situation. In other words, your strengths are also your weaknesses.

Spend some time thinking about your strengths and why they will help you to be successful in the new position. Then consider what situations might cause each strength you identified to become a weakness.

For example, being outgoing and helpful could be a strength in a job where you deal with customers every day. But being too outgoing and too helpful might mean that it takes you longer to complete certain tasks.

Similarly, being thorough and detail oriented could be a strength in a job where you analyze information, but it could also be a weakness if you spend too much time on a single detail or assignment.

By understanding your strengths, you can better articulate your weaknesses. Again, be sure that your answers are clear and concise. Be sure to practice answering these types of questions before the interview so that you are comfortable discussing your strengths and weaknesses in a straightforward way. You should be able to explain why your strengths are valuable to the new position but also demonstrate that you understand how to minimize the impact of your weaknesses.

Be sure that you are honest with the employer and yourself about your strengths and weaknesses. Remember, you don't want to just "win the job." You want to be in a situation where you enjoy your job and build a platform for a strong, continued career growth.

Brain Teasers: Some companies use brain teasers to understand your ability to problem solve, ask questions, think on your feet, and make recommendations.

- ▶ How many phone calls are made in the city of Boston per month?

- ▶ How many golf balls would fit into a in a green plastic trash can?

▶ How much dog food is used by the residents of this county on an annual basis?

Tip: First and foremost, remember the interviewer is primarily interested in your thought process and how you arrive at the answer. Take a minute to collect your thoughts, and be sure that you understand the question. Feel free to ask any pertinent clarifying questions.

Start with the macro elements first, and then drill down to the micro elements. For instance, you probably need to estimate the number of households in Boston first in order to begin to determine the number of phone calls made in the city per month.

If needed, take out your notebook, and write down the question. Begin listing the pertinent information included in the question and the steps you would take to arrive at the correct answer. Remember, the interviewer doesn't want the exact numerical answer to the question. He or she simply wants to better understand your process and the steps you will take to arrive at an answer.

To answer the question, simply walk the interviewer through the process you would use to solve the problem.

Getting-to-Know-You Questions: These questions are used to learn more about you and how you think.

- ► What is the last book you read?

- ► What is the best word to describe you?

- ► What do you like to do in your free time?

Tip: For these questions, the interviewer wants to get to know who you are, so don't answer to impress. Answer honestly, and be ready to describe the reasons.

Employee Expectations: These questions are designed to help the employer understand your expectations of the company and your new role.

- ► What are you looking for in a new company?

▶ What interests you most about this new role?

▶ Where do you see yourself in three years?

▶ What kind of training would you like to see us put into place?

▶ What other companies are you interviewing with?

▶ What questions do you have for us?

▶ What are your salary expectations?

▶ How soon can you start?

Tip: Be sure that you understand what you are really looking for in a new career and company so that you can discuss it with the interviewer and assess whether the opportunity is right for you. Before the interview, write down questions you want the employer to answer, and be ready to talk about your vision for your career and future. Consider your salary expectations and when you will be available to start your new job. Taking the time to detail these answers before the interview will help to expedite the process and ensure that you can effectively evaluate options.

Unexpected Questions: Because of the spontaneous nature of interviews, you won't know everything that is going to be asked.

If you are surprised by a random question and are not sure how to answer, stay calm and answer honestly. If you need a little time to collect your thoughts, you can ask a clarifying question, ask the interviewer to repeat the question or simply repeat the question back to the interviewer before answering. Try to avoid using stall words to fill the space like "uh" or "um." Just let the silence fill the space. Silence is fine during an interview, so you should get used to it. If you often use fill words, you can practice with a friend, family member, classmate, or acquaintance in a mock interview.

As mentioned previously, this list is in no way comprehensive, but it should give you a sense of possible question types and help you to think through how your experience, qualifications, and other skill sets relate to the new role.

As you work through pre-interview questions and prepare for your first interview, you can get some great practice by answering questions with a friend, family member, classmate, or acquaintance. For this exercise, you can give the practice questions to your family member, friend, classmate, or acquaintance and let them ask you the questions in any order they want. This will help you become more comfortable before the actual interview. It's important to practice and hear yourself answer the questions so that you can get comfortable with the process. This way, if you struggle with any of the questions or feel like the answers sound unclear or disorganized, you can adjust before the actual interview.

As you build your confidence and get more comfortable with the process, let your practice interviewer add his or her own questions and follow-ups to your responses. This will add some variety and spontaneity to better replicate the actual interview process while you practice.

Once you begin your real interviews with real companies, you should take a few minutes during or immediately after each interview to quickly jot down questions. You should make note of the questions that were asked of you that you didn't expect and those that were tough to answer. You will be interviewing with multiple companies while you narrow down your choices, and doing this will help you to better prepare for your next interview.

Some companies will require you to interview with multiple people separately and may ask for several follow-up interviews as they narrow their candidate choices. Taking notes during or immediately after each interview can be particularly helpful because companies that use multiple interviews and interviewers may ask the same or very similar questions.

CHAPTER NINE

CONNECTING

NOW THAT YOU UNDERSTAND question categories, it is important that you understand how to effectively connect with an interviewer. "Connecting" begins when two people truly understand each other's viewpoint. It is the first step in building trust and eventually creates mutual understanding. You have probably experienced what it's like to connect at different points in your life. Maybe this happened in a conversation with a friend or family member while trying to solve a problem. The moment when you and the other person suddenly understood each other, you were connecting.

Connecting is critically important during any conversation where you need to reach a decision point. An interview is a place where you definitely need to connect with the interviewer so that you can understand what he or she is looking for and he or she can understand what you are looking for.

The first step to connecting is to listen. Let the other person talk, and be sure that you understand exactly what he or she is asking. Don't interrupt, but if you are even a little unclear, pause for a moment and then ask a clarifying question. Asking questions shows the person that you are listening and genuinely interested in answering the question he or she asked.

The second step is providing adequate information. After answering a question, look for signs that the interviewer is satisfied with the type of response you gave. It is very possible that the phrasing of the question he or she asked meant one thing to the interviewer and a completely different thing to you. When this happens, you and the interviewer move further from mutual understanding, the interviewer won't get the information he or she is seeking, and you may miss an opportunity to demonstrate value. If you are not sure about the read on his or her reaction, simply ask, "Does that answer the question?"

"Does that make sense?" By doing so you can be sure that the interviewer got the type of response he or she was looking for. If not, it will give the interviewer an opportunity to rephrase the question.

Step three, be interesting. Step back from the canned answers, and give some context to who you really are. Canned answers are boring and push you and the interviewer further from connecting. Think about the interests you have, and relate them to the job you are applying for. If you like sports, music, or the outdoors, talk about why your experiences in those areas make you a stronger "fit" for the company. For example, I played football in college. If I were applying for a job where teamwork was important, I could reference a situation where through teamwork we were able to pull out a fourth quarter win.

Interests You Have That Relate to the Job and Why?

1. _____

2. _____

3. _____

4. _____

5. _____

6. _____

7. _____

In situations where an interviewee has little work experience, these kinds of "interest related" experiences give the interviewer something he or she can work with. The interviewer could then ask:

▸ "How did you get the team to pull together?"

▸ "Did you like the leadership style of your coach, why or why not?"

▸ "What do you think led to your success that time?"

Positioning interests puts you in a "human" context, adds depth to you as a potential employee, and allows the employer options for questions that will allow him or her to assess "fit."

As we discussed in the last chapter, during the interview, employers will ask you for any questions that you may have. This is an opportunity for you to further connect and ask questions that give you a clearer picture of what you are getting into with this new company. The questions you prepared before the interview can also be used to highlight some of the things you learned about the company before the interview. You should also note questions that you develop during the interview so that you can ask about them later. A few examples of this are:

▸ "I noticed that the company's growth last year was 15 percent. How did this market compare to the national growth?"

▸ "You mentioned a training program. Can you tell me a little more about that?"

▸ "What does a typical day look like for someone in this position?"

▸ How does this role help to support the overall vision of the business?

Questions like these will help you get a better understanding of the position and also show the interviewer that you have done your homework, listened to what he or she said during the interview, and have a genuine interest in making the right decision, not just "winning the job."

Questions for the Interviewer

1. _____

2. _____

3. _____

4. _____

5. _____

Be sure to follow up after the interview. It is fine to write an e-mail to employers thanking them for the opportunity to interview; however, a handwritten thank you note can be a great way to differentiate you from other candidates. You may want to incorporate relevant topics that you discussed with the interviewer to personalize your thank you note.

CHAPTER TEN

SO MANY OPTIONS

NOW THAT YOU UNDERSTAND the interviewing process, be sure that you interview with as many companies as possible. There are a few advantages when you successfully interview with several companies. One obvious advantage is receiving multiple offers. Receiving more offers, provides more choices, and with more choices, you may gain some negotiating leverage. The biggest overall advantage to fielding multiple offers is that it gives you an opportunity to look more closely at each opportunity and choose the one that is right for you. There are some basics steps that you should take when dealing with multiple offers to ensure that you are fair to each company while you allow yourself some time to make the best decision possible.

Step One: Thank each potential employer for the opportunity and offer. You need to be genuine in your appreciation. It is a lot of work for a company to conduct interviews, weigh candidate options, put together an offer, and get all the approvals and paperwork done.

Step Two: Ask the employer for some time to make your decision. You should reiterate your excitement about the opportunity, but let them know that there are several companies who have made offers and you want to ensure that you make the right choice. They may ask what others are offering you. Answering generically is a good approach. You could say something like, "Each company has provided a very competitive offer, but I need to look more closely at the specifics of each."

Step Three: If the employer simply says, "Ok, I understand that this is a big decision. Let us know by next week what you decide," then you can thank them and move on. However, if the employer asks, "What will it take to get you to sign with us right now," you have a choice; you can give them an answer and make a decision, or you can stall them. To stall, simply say, "I really want to make sure I evaluate everything. I will call you by next Thursday and let you know where I stand." The employer may simply say ok, or they may press you for an immediate decision. If pressed, you can simply revert back to your previous statement and ask for a little time.

Some employers want to quickly weed through candidates so that they don't get stuck waiting for a few weeks on someone just to find out that the candidate will choose another company. When this happens, many of the other top candidates interviewed may not still be on the market and the company will have to start the process all over again. Most companies will give you a little extra time to decide, but the top companies won't wait around long because they have a strong pool of candidates who want to work for them.

Step Four: Evaluating which company to choose is the fun part. You should first look back at your company and job list and compare your options. You should look at the attributes of each opportunity: your overall career path, the company's financial strength, its corporate culture, your job function, compensation, benefits, location, and of course, any other areas that are important to your decision.

Step Five: Create a chart with the companies at the top and the attributes down the left side. Mark each of the companies that have the things that you want and rank the companies from first place to last place.

Chart of Offers and Attributes

Attributes	Companies		
	1. Company	2. Company	3. Company
A. Location	X		X
B.			
C.			
D.			
E.			
F.			

Now, call the top company first and begin your negotiations. You want to choose the top company first because unlike in the interview process where you have a lot of time to develop and get comfortable, the negotiation process is time sensitive. The top companies are likely interviewing many other capable candidates that like the company and may accept any offer the company extends to them. You need your top company to know how interested you are immediately. If they don't hear from you for several days, they may just move on to their next top choice.

It's not out of the realm of possibility that you reach an agreement with your top choice after a phone call. If the top company is not your first phone call, you may unfairly prevent the other companies who extended offers to you from moving on to extend offers to other candidates. It is a simple courtesy to allow the companies you do not intend to choose to move on and offer other candidates the job.

Step Six: Negotiation with each company is not realistic if you have a lot of offers and you don't want to lead companies on. Chances are you will have to sacrifice some things for other things regardless of the company that you choose. Decide what is most important, and call the first company. Explain that you really appreciate the opportunity and you would like to sign with them, but you need them to look at a few items. The items could be salary, stock, stock options, retirement contribution, signing bonus, continued education, etc. If they tell you that they have no room to negotiate, then you may want to tell them that you will have a decision for them after you speak with the other companies. Be sure to thank them again for the opportunity, and then move to the next company on the list. If they say that they will take a look at the items and get back to you, then ask for a date and time when you will talk again.

Try to negotiate down the list one at a time. It may seem like a good idea to pit every company against each other and see who comes back with the best offer, but that can put you in a position where you burn bridges in the industry where you will be working. The best approach is to try first to reach a win-win with the top company on your list because you are both interested in reaching an agreement and you have both determined that there is a good "fit". If the top company won't negotiate, you can either accept their terms or move on to your next choice.

Step Seven: Choose the company that makes the most sense. Sign the offer letter, and make sure that the deal is done. Tell the company where you will be working that you will inform the other companies that you have made a decision. Once the deal is secure, tell the other companies of your decision, and thank them for the opportunity and the time they put into the process. If you are professional and grateful, many of the companies may offer to stay in touch with you in case you ever decide to make a move.

Step Eight: Fill out the paperwork with your new company, and spend a little time talking with the hiring manager to begin an open dialogue. You will want to confirm your first day, your training schedule, dress attire, and what materials to bring. While you are talking with the new manager, ask him or her about the company's vision and how your role will help accomplish the vision. This not only gives you insight into the company's vision and the way they think, but it will also solidify in the manager's mind the value of your role and remind him of why attention to your training is critical to the company's overall success. It is important to get a lot of support in your new role. Since everything will be brand new and learning will take time, it is important for the manager and/or training staff to understand the value of your role. It would be pointless for you to tell them about your value since you know very little about the true value of your role to the organization at this point. Telling them would seem awkward and may even give them the wrong impression. By asking what your role is, you seem ready to be a team player and don't accidently make yourself appear arrogant.

CHAPTER ELEVEN

FIRST, SECOND, AND THIRD IMPRESSIONS

ONCE YOU HAVE BEEN HIRED, there are several things to consider before you begin your first day. The next several chapters are designed to help familiarize you with your new environment and help you to create plans to facilitate continued success in your new career.

As you begin your new career, every day will provide you the opportunity to add value to your personal brand. Adding value to your brand will help you with the tangible elements of your career such as promotions, salary negotiation, and finding new opportunities for growth within your field.

Your first interactions with people in your new role are critically important. People will instantly begin to categorize you. If you appear arrogant, shy, loud, or silly, then that will be the way you are viewed in the office for a while. You need to understand that the moment you walk in the door you are being judged, and your actions affect the value of your personal brand. You should be polite, enthusiastic, helpful, and appreciative of everyone you meet regardless of his or her title, position, etc. You never know who the true influencers are in a new job.

During training, it is important to excel at everything you are given to learn. Spend extra time to be sure you understand all of the information you are receiving. Ask questions of the trainer and other employees when needed, but be sure not to overburden the employees around you. While you are training, there is very little to measure your success other than your ability to learn. Since many companies have a lot of individual online training now, it is important to periodically update your manager on your success. You should schedule a little time each week to discuss your progress with your training staff and/or manager. By taking the initiative to set the meetings, you will show the employer that you are a self-starter and that you take the training seriously. The update will also give you an opportunity to "connect" with the manager or trainer and understand what is most important to him or her. Some managers may not have time each week, but simply suggesting the meeting will differentiate you from other trainees.

CHAPTER TWELVE
PLANNING FOR SUCCESS

PUTTING TOGETHER A PLAN for your career is very important to becoming successful in the future. When you have a documented career plan rather than a few thoughts in your head, you will have a much clearer path to track your progress and plan your success. Throughout your new career, you will be able to refer back to the plan and add new details. When you are putting the plan together, the first section to consider is the goals section. These should be both professional and personal goals. Take a look back at the questions you answered in the first section of the book about your goals.

▶ Write down long and short term goals.

A. _____

B. _____

C. _____

D. _____

E. _____

▶ Write down the big picture things that will need to happen for you to accomplish your goals.

A. _____

B. _____

C. _____

D. _____

E. _____

▸ Now consider the specific steps you will need to take to accomplish those goals.

A. _____

B. _____

C. _____

D. _____

E. _____

▸ Once you understand the steps, add in timelines for completion.

A. _____

B. _____

C. _____

D. _____

E. _____

▶ Add in what you will need to do this year, month, week, and day to meet your goals.

A. _____

B. _____

C. _____

D. _____

E. _____

▶ Now list the items that may prevent you from accomplishing these goals.

A. _____

B. _____

C. _____

D. _____

E. _____

▶ Think about what additional steps you could take to ensure successful completion of your goals.

A. _____

B. _____

C. _____

D. _____

E. _____

Now you should have a road map of what you will need to accomplish each day to successfully build your personal brand and reach your goals. Think about this planning document as a living, breathing document that you can always refer to and update with new goals and actions. That way it evolves as your career evolves.

Once your goal planning is done, you should put together a daily tasking list. This list will be based on your daily goals and include the specific actions that you will need to accomplish in order to achieve your daily goals. The daily task list will have "to do" items that can be added or crossed off each day.

A. _____

B. _____

C. _____

D. _____

E. _____

CHAPTER THIRTEEN
EXECUTION

NOW THAT YOU HAVE a plan in place, you need to execute the plan. Execution will make the difference in your success or failure. Every day, you will move closer to or further from accomplishing your overall goals. If you work harder and smarter, you will move closer. Here are a few tips to keep in mind when working toward building a successful career.

- ▸ *Stay on task, and focus on mastering your job.* Measure your own performance each day, and don't waste time. Think about the goals of the organization and your own personal goals, and be sure you are spending time on things that make progress toward these goals. It is easy to get side tracked by something that is "quasi" important or something that is more "fun" but is of little value. For example, don't be the waiter choosing to fold napkins for dinner while your lunch customers are waiting for drink refills. It could be argued that the napkins need to get folded some time before dinner, but if doing so would dramatically affect your performance during lunch, then focusing on the task at hand with the revenue generating customers is most important at the time.

▶ *Always learn everything you can.* Continued learning should occur for the rest of your life if you want to become truly successful. Depending on the company, there may be online learning modules, webinars, or classes available to you that you can assign yourself and take at your convenience. It is important to always evaluate your own learning needs and not wait for someone else to tell you what to do. Ask about additional opportunities that the company offers for continuing education. A top performer with a great command of information can be very valuable to any company, so be sure to take the initiative.

▸ *Work on building professional relationships with others.* While achieving your own goals, lend a hand to help others accomplish their goals. You should always keep your eye on your own performance and be sure that you achieve your own goals, but developing a strong network of teammates can multiply your ability to achieve. Internal and external resources can add a lot of value through collaborative goal achievement, so be sure to understand the motivations and needs of your teammates, and offer help when you can.

▸ *Be Punctual.* Tardiness may give the impression that you don't care. If you plan to be fifteen minutes early always, you will rarely be late. Meetings, training, events, etc. are opportunities to interact with others and develop your skills and career, so be sure to be early so that you have a little time to socialize before the event begins. If you are early to the office, you may get some time to learn something new, reflect on the day, or just collect your thoughts before work.

▶ *Be Responsive.* Unresponsiveness can often be perceived as a lack of interest or initiative. Return calls and emails quickly. If you don't have an answer but you plan to work on getting the answer, return the call and explain. If you don't return the call, the other person may feel like you are ignoring them or that you are unreliable. When you have a lot of emails or phone calls to return, take a second and prioritize. Respond to the most urgent, important communications first, and then respond to the others. Twenty-four hours may be acceptable for less urgent responses, but in many cases people expect an answer within a couple of hours or less. Be sure to stay on top of communication. It makes a big difference.

▶ *Make good choices.* Remember, building a successful career is a long-term process. Making a snap decision that lacks thought is a bad idea. Think through the long-term effects of each decision, and don't burn bridges unnecessarily. Making solid big picture decisions will help you to achieve long-term success.

▶ *Reflect.* To be truly effective in building a successful career requires time for reflection each day. Think about your progress toward reaching your goals. Consider what you may need to do differently, and make the appropriate changes to your plan and task list. Daily reflection will allow you to make appropriate modifications as needed to reach your goals.

▶ *Spend time each day learning about the field you are in.* Read articles, blogs, and trade magazines to stay in the know. You should be able to reference material you have read when talking with others in your industry. If you take your career seriously, others will too.

▸ *Ask for feedback.* You can create a healthy dialogue with your manager, team members, employees, and internal and external resources by asking for regular feedback. Be sure to listen and make the appropriate adjustments. By doing so, you can dramatically increase your overall effectiveness and reach within the organization.

Staying out of the fray is important. You don't want to get sidetracked with things that dilute your ability to reach your goals. A few tips for in and out of the office include:

▸ *Politics.* Stay out of the politics of the office. Don't gossip, stand around and listen to gossip, or make fun of others in the office.

▸ *Jokes.* Avoid jokes that could be perceived even remotely as insulting to anyone in or out of the office. There is specific compliance information that your company should give you about employee interaction and what is and isn't appropriate and legal in the office.

▶ *Avoid personal relationships in the office.* It is important to remember that the people you work with are not the same as your longtime friends from home or school. People may circulate personal information about you if given the opportunity, and many employees may see you as competition in the office and would take any available opportunity to get ahead. Be sure not to reveal any information in the office that you don't want everyone in the office to know. Regardless of how well you think you know a colleague, he or she probably knows someone else better, so keep your important personal information close.

▶ *Keep an upbeat attitude.* It is important to always be upbeat and display a great attitude while working. If you appear to be down at work often, people may wrongly believe that you are upset about work or that you are unhappy with your new job. Maintain a cheery demeanor whenever possible.

▸ *Be enthusiastic.* You should be enthusiastic about the company and your new opportunity regardless of who you are speaking with. Customers, vendors, other divisions, and even friends may be connected in some way to people at your new job. Be sure to display enthusiasm so that your new employer is constantly reminded of your positive energy.

▸ *Don't post negative information about work on social media.* Social media can be a great tool for meeting people and making new connections, but you should expect anything you post online to be seen by others. It is a good idea to avoid posting negative info about work on your pages. If there is something that really bothers you, you may want to find another job where you will be happy.

▸ *Dress professionally.* Dressing professionally is important in the office. Don't wear clothing that is inappropriate for your environment. You should look at what the dress policy is at work and follow it. If you want to dress a little nicer than the minimum requirement, don't overdo it because you will seem like you are trying too hard and this may disconnect you from your colleagues.

- *Happy hours.* Happy hours are simply offsite employee functions. If you attend these functions, stay professional just as you would in the office. Try not to stay too long at these functions, and don't engage in gossip before, during, or after the function.

- *Congratulate others on their successes.* Be sure to take a minute to congratulate others when they are successful. It shows that you care and will help you to develop a better rapport with teammates.

- *Don't publically discuss other people's failures.* Regardless of the situation, nothing good comes out of being vocal about someone's failure. If you must give someone negative feedback, do it one-on-one, privately.

The big takeaway from this section is to stay focused on achieving your goals. Once you have a plan and task list completed, execute. Take the time to reflect and reevaluate, and always keep learning.

CHAPTER FOURTEEN

SELLING GREAT IDEAS

REGARDLESS OF WHICH CAREER you have chosen, sales skills will be an important part of your success. Selling ideas to other employees, managers, and internal and external resources is a big part of any business professional's job. It's important to understand the process and what is truly important to each conversation. We will cover some common scenarios and examples to illustrate the right and wrong way to sell. Listening, connecting, and reaching a clear and mutual understanding is as critical here as it was during the interviewing process. If you find that you need more detail on consultative selling and professional selling, please consider reading my book, *Become Relevant*.

As you get further into your career, you will have improvement ideas. These ideas often can be very helpful to a business, but they must be presented in a way that helps others connect with the value of the idea. Some people have a tendency to get excited about an idea and talk for a long time about the value of the idea. The problem is that most people listening have a short attention span and will lose interest in listening after about 30 seconds. When this happens, your great points will be lost because your audience will just tune you out and think about whatever they want for a few minutes until you are done talking. Here is an example of the first approach:

Ask a question. "Why are we unable to hire another account manager to help us sell more into our account base and increase our business this year?"

Listen to the answer. "The current account managers can handle what we have, and we don't really need the added stress of hiring new...."

You immediately launch into the solution and cut off the speaker. "I think we could get it all done if we really spent some time to get the right person for the job. I could find someone and hire them. That way you could avoid the stress of hiring. I have lots of experience finding good people, and my experience and contacts will really help us to locate the right person. You really should let me put this together for you since it will help the company meet its goals and allow us to grow our business. I think we could have this person really make a difference in the company, and it would be great!"

"No way; not right now. There are too many problems with it."

You launch right back into it. "But I think that if you just give me a chance to find the right person, we will really be able to get someone that makes all of us more successful and..."

At this point, the person you are talking to is thinking about what they need to pick up for dinner after work and what they want to watch on TV tonight. They may be pretending to check emails, or they may even get a call they need to take.

In sales, this is called the "show up and throw up approach." It is what happens when you try to simply "tell" your ideas and force the other person to say yes. Saying yes should not be the goal. Just like before when we talked about interviewing, "winning," should not be the goal. The goal should be to reach a mutual understanding of the situation, issue, and solution, and then move forward with a resolution.

One simple principle of sales is that you must "listen and ask questions" for most of the conversation. It seems counterintuitive to listen and ask questions rather than talk, but remember the goal of the conversation. To reach mutual understanding, you must truly understand the other person, their obstacles, and their ideas on resolution. To do this you need to listen.

Often the person you are talking with doesn't really understand the situation because he or she hasn't had time to think it through. That means that he or she needs to actually consider the situation which is why questions are much more effective than statements.

You both must completely understand the situation and obstacles before you can offer a solution. If you create a mutual understanding, then you will both develop a desire to reach a solution together. If your idea is a good one, that solves all of the issues, the other person will be much more apt to agree to your idea.

To effectively "sell" your ideas, you need to apply some basic sales concepts to your process. Here is what a basic process for selling should look like. Here is the same situation as above with a very different result:

Ask a question. "Why are we unable to hire another account manager to help us sell more into our account base and increase our business this year?"

Listen to the answer. "The current account managers can handle what we have, and we don't really need the added stress of hiring new people. Plus the new account managers would probably be expensive, and the existing account managers would be mad if they had to give up accounts."

Repeat the key points. "Ok, so it would be stressful to hire someone new, they would be expensive, and our existing account managers would not want to give up accounts."

Check for a mutual understanding. "Is that right?"

"Yes. That's right."

Ask about the effect of non-resolution. "What will happen if we don't grow our business this year?"

"We will probably have to cut two positions."

Repeat the effect. "So we will lose two positions?"

"Yes"

Ask about the options. "What options do we have to increase revenues?"

"We need to get our people selling more into the existing accounts, and we need them to generate new business development. We have a headcount to add a person, but I am afraid we won't grow, and then we will need to cut three people."

Repeat the key options. "So, we need to sell to existing and new business accounts, and we have a headcount to hire another person?" Ask about your idea: "What if I found a new business development person instead of an account manager for a reasonable price, and they only sold to incremental new business accounts?"

Listen. "Well that might work, but no one is going to be affordable and only want to work on new accounts."

Ask clarifying questions. "What is affordable for us right now?"

"X thousand per year."

State your solution idea. "I would like the opportunity to find a person that will work for less than X thousand per year who is solely focused on new business."

Listen to concerns. "You are not going to find that out there."

Ask clarifying questions "Why do you believe I won't be able to find someone?"

"You won't, they don't exist. Even if you find someone, who will train them?"

Ask for the opportunity to work toward reaching an agreement. "I will find this person and let you interview them. Then, I can train them if you will agree to use the open headcount."

"Fine, if you find and train them, I will get the headcount."

This approach allows both of you to reach a solution together. The manager may not be completely convinced that the approach will work, but he or she wants to find a solution. Fully aware of the situation and what will happen to the business if a solution is not found to the issue, the manager looks to you for help. This approach has made finding the right solution a joint effort rather than something that only one person is committed to.

CHAPTER FIFTEEN
SELLING YOURSELF

SELLING YOURSELF is a little different than selling your ideas. Because you don't want to appear
to be a shameless self-promoter, you need to use
some tact in the sale. There are several situations
you will face where you will need to sell yourself:

- *Selling one-on-one for a raise.* If you are in a
  one-on-one conversation with your manager,
  selling for a raise is simply another negotiation.
  Your leverage is that you can always leave, and
  their leverage is that they believe you won't
  leave. Some people approach this conversation
  the wrong way by threatening to leave. If you
  choose that route, you need to be prepared

to walk out the door and collect your things because you may be told, "Ok leave." That's why a better approach is to understand what your manager expects of you before you walk into the negotiation. If you are conducting the weekly or bi-weekly meetings with your manager, you should have a good sense of expectations. Before you walk into the meeting, prepare notes and figures on everything you have done that has exceeded expectations. Prepare a bulleted list that the manager can quickly look at to see specific items that have improved your area of responsibility. Also include items that have contributed to the success of the overall business.

► *When you are talking about a raise, your personal financial issues are the least important part of the conversation closely followed by your feelings.* What is most important is to lay out a case which shows your contribution level exceeds your compensation. This case should be based on facts so that anyone could look at it and decide that you should be given a raise. Here is an example of both types of conversations. Think about what your decision would be if you were a manager with a very limited budget for raises for all employees.

SCENARIO ONE:

You: "I wanted to talk to you about a pay increase."

Manager: "Ok."

You: "I need a raise because I have lots of bills: car, apartment, school loans. I need to make more money, and I felt like you would understand, so I wanted to talk to you."

Manager: "I can't do anything right now to help you. I'm sorry."

You: "Well, I'm going to have to get another job at night just to pay my bills if I don't get some more money."

Manager: "Well, do what you have to do. You do have a bright future here, but I can't do anything right now to help you out."

You: "Well, I got a call from a recruiter yesterday, and they said that they had an opportunity that would pay me ten percent more."

Manager: "Well, I'd hate to lose you, but I understand you need to do what's best for you. We only do increases every two years, so we can talk again in six months."

SCENARIO TWO:

You: "I wanted to talk to you about a pay increase."

Manager: "Ok."

You: "I pulled this info for you to look at." Hand the paper to the manager and pause for a second.

Manager: "Wow, ok, what is this?"

You: "It is an executive summary of the steps I have taken that have contributed to a 22 percent increase in productivity within my group. I also included some of the other contributions I have made to the overall growth of the business. The overall business has increased by 12 percent, and I believe we can continue that trend."

Manager: "Wow, this is very impressive."

You: "Thanks. Based on our overall numbers, I estimate these changes have saved us close to three million dollars and increased our revenues by over seven million."

Manager: "Well, you certainly put together some impressive information here."

You: "Given the savings of 3 million and the revenue increase of 7 million, I have positively affected the business by over 10 million dollars. I would like to get my compensation in line with my contribution."

Manager: "Well, we have limited money in the budget for raises; I would like to do something to help you but I'm not sure what my boss will approve."

You: "I understand the limited budget, but I would think you would have a strong case for an increase with the info I have given you. Would it make sense for us to talk to your boss together?"

Manager: "No, I'll handle it. What kind of increase are we talking about?"

In scenario one, the conversation was based on things that didn't directly bring value to the business, so the first conversation was about the manager helping the employee. The second scenario was based on the value brought to the business and based on tangible benefits to the business. If you want to increase your pay, you need to position your value to the business first so that the conversation is about the business first and you second. Always base your conversations on value to the business because if you are a valuable asset to the business, the manager will want to keep you motivated to continue being valuable. Often managers won't really be aware of your contributions or haven't considered the true value that you bring, so it is up to you to remind them and detail the logic of the increase.

- ▶ *Subtly selling to set up for a raise or promotion.* Subtle selling should occur every day. To do this, you need to time the conversation correctly. You should only bring up quick bits of information to remind people of your value at the appropriate times. This technique is more effective because it is not a long drawn out conversation where you look like a self-promoter. Quick casual reminders can be very effective in detailing your value as a contributor. Here are a few examples.

  Manager: "We exceeded out targets this month!"

You: "By how much?"

Manager: "25%."

You: "I wonder how much the new sales person we hired to sell new business accounts contributed."

Manager: "It looks like she was seventy-five percent of the increase."

You: "Great, we have been doing weekly meetings and calls to new customers together. If she has increased the business that much so far, I'm excited to see how much we can improve the business next month."

Manager: "Me too!"

You: "I have been spending three hours a week teaching her my process, but I think with that kind of success, I will spend four hours a week with her."

Manager: "That would be great! You are really doing a great job with her. Keep it up."

This kind of conversation is great because it reminds the manager of your contribution and how it directly affects the overall goals of the organization and directly benefits him or her. It is important not to "tell" because again "telling" is less valuable. The conversation where the manager needs to consider everything you are discussing and respond to you with tangible value based answers makes a big difference. This is the type of information that you can reference on your executive summary during a performance review or pay increase discussion:

- ▶ *Selling value to a group.* To cover this complex and dynamic concept it is recommended that you read my book, *Become Relevant,* for detailed information on how to effectively sell to a group.

- ▶ *Selling others.* Whether you are trying to sell as a manager or you are selling an idea to another colleague, you will need to be able to sell others on completing tasks. As previously stated, "telling" someone to do something is very ineffective. They may do it, but if they don't believe doing the task is valuable to them, they will just go through the motions and not really complete the task effectively. If you are a manager, selling employees is almost the same process you used before when selling your manager on an idea. However, unlike that situation, you must leave the conversation with the employee completely buying into the implementation of the idea. When you were selling to your manager, you were completing the implementation of hiring someone so the only person who needed to believe in completing the task was you. When you leave the conversation and you need another employee to do something, he or she is the one who needs to complete the task; therefore, he or she must buy in.

Here is an example of the process:

Ask a question. "What do we need to do to get those reports out?"

Listen to the answer. "I need to pull the data first and then put it together, but I'm swamped right now."

Repeat the key points. "Ok, so you still need to pull the data and put it together but you are too busy." Check for a mutual understanding. "Is that right?"

"Yes. That's right."

Ask about the effect of non-resolution. "What will happen if we don't get the reports out?"

"We will probably all be looking for new jobs since the report is for the CEO."

Repeat the effect. "Ok, so we will all be looking for new jobs?"

"Probably! I'm so stressed out!"

Ask about the options. "What options do we have?"

"None! I am the only one who can pull the data, and I am stuck here at the reception desk since Dave is out. The phone won't stop ringing, and I have to log every call in the system!"

Repeat the key options. "So, you are the only one who can pull the data, and you have to answer phones for Dave and log calls?" Ask about your idea. "What if I answer calls and log them in the system for you while you focus on getting the report done?"

Listen. "Well that might work, but no one else knows how to log calls, and it would take me a month to teach you."

Ask clarifying questions. "Do the calls need to be logged as they come in, or could they be logged at the end of the day or tomorrow?"

"It is just for sales leads, so they can be logged whenever."

"Are there any compliance or other legal issues with logging the calls the next day, rather than right away?"

"No, there are no compliance or legal issues as this is simply something I track to help provide information to the sales reps."

State your solution idea. "Ok, how about I answer the calls and write down the info in Excel, and then you can log them tomorrow after the deadline for the report to the CEO. That way we can all keep our jobs."

Listen to concerns. "Maybe, but you don't even know where to transfer people."

Ask clarifying questions "Why can't I just use the extension list?"

"I guess that would work."

Ask for the opportunity to work toward reaching an agreement. "Ok, can we make this work, so we can get the report done?"

"Sure, but let me know if you get stuck, ok?"

"No problem. Can you definitely get that report done?"

"I'll do it; I guess it is the most important thing we can do today."

"Well besides losing our job, our CEO needs the info to get funding from the bank so we can expand our bank lines. That will make the difference between the business's success and failure next year."

"Wow, I didn't realize that!"

"Yes, so your report matters a lot."

"I'm on it right now."

This scenario is typical in any field; people often don't prioritize and just do what is in front of them. You will often have to convince someone to do something, but simply telling him or her will not be effective. You need to first connect and reach a mutual understanding of the issues. Once you both understand the issue, you can work toward a resolution. If you don't ask questions, you will not have a clear view of the whole situation, and without posing questions, the person you are talking with may not have thought about the situation and the implications of non-resolution.

- ▸ *Pointing out others' faults subtly.* To point out faults subtly requires tact and discretion. It is important to not publically point out shortcomings. If you have to do so, the best way of handling the conversation is to offer a theoretical reason for the other person not doing something. This way you are not saying, "He is a slacker!" or "She doesn't care whether she is late to work!" or "He doesn't mind being average!"

  A way to point out shortcomings without passing judgment could look like this:

  "With the work load everyone has this week, he probably had more pressing things to do."

  or "The construction on the interstate has made traffic unbearable. I bet she will be here soon,"

  or "He always seems so content."

By pointing out the shortcomings in a positive way, you don't look like you are trying to point them out. The other person to whom you are talking can then choose to accept the theoretical reason, or read between the lines. Either way, you should not do this often and only when necessary.

▶ *Defending against others pointing out your faults.* If someone attacks you in a public meeting or any type of public setting and looks to you for a response, it can be very uncomfortable for everyone in the room. The best way to handle the situation is to immediately end the public discussion and take it "offline." If you just take it offline though, people will assume it is true. A quick response first may be appropriate to maintain continuity of the conversation before the comment. One way to do this is as follows:

Attacker: "Well, your team took forever to get the report to the CEO. We almost lost our bank line!"

You: Smile confidently; "You don't have all of the information; I think this discussion is outside the context of this conversation, so let's discuss it privately."

The attacker should choose to accept your response particularly if the comment is outside the context of the conversation, but if he or she doesn't, you may need to respond. If you need to discuss the issue in front of others, succinctly address the issue. Be sure to be unemotional and simply list the facts.

Attacker: "Well, I think this is the appropriate venue and audience for discussion."

You: Smile and reply, "Sure, we were two people short in the office that day and needed to shuffle responsibilities to get it done. We did that and got the report out on time. It required some overtime, and I had to answer phones in addition to my other responsibilities, but the team pulled together well, and we got the bank line." Then you should smile proudly.

This should thwart the attacker but if it doesn't, you may need to simply cut the conversation off.

Attacker: "Well, you could have started sooner!"

You: "Well, I'm sure we can all make improvements. Let's not waste everyone's time on this issue. I'll be available after the meeting if you have additional suggestions."

That response needs to be firm. If done correctly, the attacker will look like he is wasting everyone's time by trying to call you out on something that is irrelevant.

CHAPTER SIXTEEN

CONCLUSION

I WANTED TO KEEP this book short and to the point. Remember to always listen, connect, and develop a mutual understanding with those around you regardless of what you are doing.

- ► From interviewing to management, connecting to develop a mutual understanding is the most important skill one can develop.

- ► From interviewing to selling ideas, always take some time to prepare and develop a solid plan.

▶ Don't forget to ask questions, and never simply tell people what to do when you are trying to convince them of your opinion.

▶ Never stop learning, and continue to reflect everyday on your personal and professional goals.

ABOUT THE AUTHOR

B ILL HOBBS has won the top performance awards as an account executive and as a manager in two Fortune 500 companies. He is a co-inventor with an active patent and the founder of two companies. As a consultant and advisor, Bill enjoys working with tech companies as they shape visions to build successful businesses. Bill's unique blend of Fortune 500 and startup experience provides new approaches to help founders refine ideas and develop innovative models for sustained growth. From interviewing new employees to his experience as a P&L manager and a coach, Bill has unique insight into the challenges that business professionals face every day.

Drawing from his business knowledge, Bill wrote *The WORK Book* which encourages students to work early and often with teachers, career counselors, faculty advisors, and professors to build their personal brands. *The WORK Book* has now become required reading at several top universities around the country.

Bill also enjoys working within the arts and volunteering.